PUBLIC LANDS, PUBLIC HERITAGE
THE NATIONAL FOREST IDEA

√

PUBLIC LANDS, PUBLIC HERITAGE
THE NATIONAL FOREST IDEA

Alfred Runte

**with Guest Essay by Harold K. Steen
and photographs by David Muench**

1991
ROBERTS RINEHART PUBLISHERS
in cooperation with
THE BUFFALO BILL HISTORICAL CENTER

Copyright © 1991 by the Buffalo Bill Historical Center
Published by Roberts Rinehart Publishers
Post Office Box 666 Niwot, Colorado 80544
International Standard Book Number 0–911797–94–7
Library of Congress Catalog Card Number 91–060435
Printed in the United States of America

Book and cover design by Richard Firmage

Front cover art: W. Herbert Dunton, *The Forest Ranger*; oil on canvas, 32″x22″;
Courtesy of Mr. and Mrs. Kenn S. George.

Frontispiece: Hans Kleiber, *The Lone Fisherman*; etching, 11¾″x8¾″; courtesy
of Buffalo Bill Historical Center, gift of Lucille M. Wright.

Back cover: Karl Bodmer, *Forest Scene on the Lehigh, Pennsylvania*, ca. 1834,
black and white aquatint; Buffalo Bill Historical Center.

Foreword

One hundred years ago, within the boundaries of the State of Wyoming and adjacent to America's first national park, Yellowstone, President Benjamin Harrison established what was to become America's first national forest. Designated the Yellowstone Park Timber Land Reserve, it spanned nearly a million and a quarter acres and became the initial physical manifestation of a sweeping new federal conservation idea. By act of Congress on March 3, 1891, the President was empowered to set aside forest reserves for the purpose of preserving, protecting, and later, managing natural resources. A century later the National Forests comprise over 191 million acres administered by an agency of more than 30,000 people.

Determining where and how this novel idea of public stewardship for public lands began and what forces have influenced its maturation over the past century is the purpose of this volume and the accompanying exhibition. This effort is part of a broader celebration of the National Forest System Centennial. Like the system itself, the exhibition has been fashioned from the union of governmental and private energies, input, and enthusiasms. The Buffalo Bill Historical Center, a private museum, and the U.S. Forest Service, a federal agency, join together to commemorate the history of the conservation ethic in America.

The joint planning for this catalog and exhibition began in June, 1987. At the urging of Steve Mealey, then Supervisor of the Shoshone National Forest, the museum and national forest representatives met to discuss the possibility of a cooperative effort. Ultimately, Rob Hendricks, Director of the National Forest Centennial Celebration, was assigned to oversee the project for the Forest Service, and Paul Fees, Senior Curator of the Historical Center, coordinated the effort for the museum. In December of 1989 the distinguished conservation historian, Alfred Runte, was brought into the project. His task was to undertake critical original research on the evolution of the national forest idea and to author the catalog while also assisting in the organization of the associated exhibition. It is to these three gentlemen that we owe our greatest measure of thanks. Further acknowledgement is happily accorded to many others who have given time and effort for the organization of this part of the National Forest Centennial celebration. We received help and advice from many people in the Forest Service and in colleges, museums, and businesses around the country. Special thanks are due Dr. Harold K. Steen, Durham, N.C.; Mark Reed, Portland, Oregon; Christy Westrup, Troutdale, Oregon; Edgar Brannon, Jr., Milford, Pennsylvania; Rita Cantu, Prescott, Arizona; Howell H. Howard, Winnetka, Illinois; Joseph A. Miller, New Haven, Connecticut; Jud Moore, Missoula, Montana; and to Sarah Boehme, Christina Stopka, Joanne Kudla, Elizabeth Holmes, Jay Wright, and Sylvia Huber of the Buffalo Bill Historical Center.

Contents

Early Forest Service exhibits, such as this overflowing display at the Lands Products Exposition, Portland, Oregon, in 1914, were unabashed checklists suggesting the patriotism, professionalism, and dedication of the agency. National Archives (95G-163556).

Preface

Early in August 1989, I received a call from Robert L. Hendricks, the director of the National Forest Centennial Celebration, U.S. Forest Service. Would I consider, he asked, accepting an invitation from the Buffalo Bill Historical Center in Cody, Wyoming, to help plan the centennial exhibit of the national forests, an exhibit scheduled to open at the center in June 1991? I agreed, and two weeks later found myself at the airport in Billings, Montana, where I joined up with Rob and his colleague E. J. "Ed" Vandermillan, the director of the Forest Service research center at Grey Towers in Milford, Pennsylvania, for the final leg of our trip down to Cody. Ed had never been to Yellowstone, so we decided to take the "long way" into Cody via the park: first heading over the Beartooth Highway, then up the Grand Canyon of the Yellowstone, then around the northeastern corner of Yellowstone Lake, and finally east out of the park through the Shoshone National Forest. That forest, Rob explained, was the reason for our being here. On March 30, 1891, large portions of it had originally been set aside by President Benjamin Harrison as the Yellowstone Park Timber Land Reserve, the very first "national forest" in the United States. Accordingly, in 1987 Steve Mealey, the Shoshone National Forest supervisor, had approached the Buffalo Bill Historical Center in neighboring Cody to host and organize something appropriate to the one-hundredth anniversary. And so it was that the center had suggested that I participate, and that Rob, Ed, and I were now taking the long way into Cody, not only to familiarize ourselves with the general location of the first national forest but also—and more to the point—to see if we might come to a preliminary understanding of just what the exhibit and this book should in fact try to say.

In retrospect, it was one of those memorable afternoons, a time for making new friends and for sharing a wealth of good ideas. Rob, I came to realize, was especially troubled by the various controversies currently embroiling the national forest system. Ed too seemed to be looking for something more than another restatement of Forest Service ideologies. Have we, they kept asking, lost something precious to our agency? Why is it that we can't seem to come together any more on the fundamental reasons for our being? How, in other words, might the centennial exhibit help us to recapture our former sense of purpose and mission?

That was, I cautioned, a very tall order. Throughout their history, the national forests have meant many different things to many different people. Even now, at the exit to every forest, a large, official sign boldly proclaims that the traveler is leaving a "Land of Many Uses." It follows that there is no single (one might say proper) definition of the national forest system. Consequently, the more Rob and Ed tried to find one, the more likely was the possibility that their own exhibit would get swept up by the tides of disagreement.

It was important, in any case, not to rework the standard definitions and, by so doing, to impose them on the exhibit, thereby simply duplicating the common "look" of so many past celebrations. What is it about government, I asked, that insists on squeezing everything in? This should not, by any means, be another agency "checklist." Above all, the exhibit should avoid the common accusation that government agencies—and especially the Forest Service—tend to cast everything in an economic light. "One basic weakness in a conservation system based wholly on economic motives," wrote the distinguished ecologist Aldo Leopold, for example, "is that most members of the land community have no economic value." Rather than admit the fact, however, Americans rushed to revise their definitions. "When one of these non-economic categories is threatened, and if we happen to love it, we invent subterfuges to give it economic importance. At the beginning of the century songbirds were supposed to be disappearing," he noted, citing a familiar illustration. "Ornithologists jumped to the rescue with some distinctly shaky evidence to the effect that insects would eat us up if birds failed to control them." The point was that "the evidence had to be economic in order to be valid."

This explains, in brief, why the national forests themselves are always in the maelstrom of controversy, and why simply redefining that controversy is not likely to be convincing. Rather we should acknowledge, from the outset, that the national forests are essentially for economic development. As Gifford Pinchot expressed that criterion in 1904, "Use must be the test by which the forester tries himself, for by it his work will inevitably be tried." Why, then, deny the fact, resorting, as has been customary over the years, to a host of modifying adjectives to soften the word *use*? Call it "wise" use or "multiple" use — it is much the same thing. But of course the public expects the Forest Service to manage the forests "wisely." The key word is still *use*, the obligation to develop the national forests not just for one but rather for a broad range of public interests.

The trouble is not the use of the forests; rather, as Aldo Leopold observed, it is the tendency to forget that many of humankind's greatest achievements have had nothing to do with economics. Where Leopold parted company with Pinchot's edict — and where others have parted since — is at the point where economics seemed to be the *only* criterion for rationalizing the necessity of the national forests. Leopold had nothing against managing resources. It was just that some resources should never be managed and that the worth of modern forestry was in having the insight to know the difference between divisible and indivisible natural values.

Dixie National Forest sign; photograph by Alfred Runte. In addition to responsible logging and the protection of critical watersheds, the national forests have come to be identified with other colorful styles of life born of America's frontier heritage, including mining, grazing, hunting, and fishing, each carefully regulated to accommodate everyone's right of access to these "lands of many uses."

Sensing my admiration for Aldo Leopold, Rob immediately inter-jected, noting that Leopold had begun his own career in the U.S. Forest Service. With an equal sense of pride, Ed seconded that observation. And suddenly, we had found a reason for true consensus. On reflection, what each of us wanted to protect was the opportunity for changing course, for taking the public lands in whatever direction the latest schol-arship or debate or national priority warranted. The larger significance of the national forests is their existence in the first place. The Forest Service can be asked to change direction because there are still forests left to change. Rather than get tempted once again to justify the agency's motives, we decided that the coming centennial should celebrate the longevity—indeed the vitality—of the forests themselves.

To be sure, the reality of the national forests is no excuse for com-placency; in the final analysis, a nation's reality merely sets its bound-aries of responsibility. Given its historical abundance, the United States has found it all too easy to evade that responsibility, to sidestep the issues by insisting that its good fortune was somehow an entitlement, part of which included the privilege of evasion. And yet, unlike so many other nations with comparable problems of exploitation, the United States is among the handful that have tried to reverse course. In just the two years since I met with Rob and Ed, another one hundred million acres of rain forests around the globe have been cut down or burned. Those countries, it follows, are losing not only their forests but also, and equally important, every remaining possibility for debating forest usage. What difference will it make to argue about preservation or develop-ment if there is nothing left to argue about?

In the United States, the debate is still possible. In the national forest system alone, the American people collectively share more than 191 million acres of land, an area nearly twice the size of the state of California. That statistic may not be reason for complacency; it does, however, grant us the privilege of feeling proud. Whatever the system's faults, it nonetheless endures as a great national proving ground, a place for testing and reevaluating that most basic question: Can use and the environment responsibly coexist?

That is where the debate begins and where many readers, I sus-pect, will feel obliged to part company. Even so, the existence of the national forests is not the point of disagreement. There is cause for cel-ebration just in recognition of the fact that American history, after all, might have gone off in another direction, depriving us, like those in the

Third World, of *both* the land and its resources. Whatever else we may have lost, we have not lost the opportunity for changing course.

A final word, then, about content. What follows is an illustration and interpretation of the national forest *idea*. When the Forest Service itself has contributed to that idea's visualization, in other words, to the depiction of national forests in art and photography, that aspect is, of course, fully recognized. As for whether the agency's management directives have been consistent and responsible, again I choose to limit myself to interpretations of the national forest *ideal*.

For the privilege, I thank the U.S. Forest Service, and especially its centennial director, Robert L. Hendricks. As I discovered two years ago, Rob is an engaging and perceptive critic. I was urged to write this book exactly as I saw fit. Rob asked only that it be fair to every reasonable interpretation, and he thus made certain, at every stage, that I had unrestricted access to the broadest range of Forest Service materials.

E. J. Vandermillan has since retired from the agency, but again, I will always be grateful for his insights on our pilgrimage through Yellowstone and the Shoshone National Forest. Rob further informs me that Steve Mealey, the Shoshone National Forest supervisor, deserves much of the credit for getting the project started in the first place. It is a pleasure to acknowledge Steve's contribution and thereby to underscore how fortunate the Forest Service has been to benefit from the vision and conviction of such dedicated public servants.

At the Buffalo Bill Historical Center, Peter H. Hassrick, director, and Dr. Paul Fees, senior curator, kept the spark of introspection and creativity alive over month after month of research and discussion. The day after our swing through Greater Yellowstone, Rob, Ed, and I joined Peter and Paul at the museum—along with a number of distinguished representatives of the U.S. Forest Service—for another day of productive brainstorming. Dr. Harold K. Steen, executive director of the Forest History Society, was also present and has since been a crucial source for a wealth of materials, including the guest essay in this volume.

The staffs of the Library of Congress, the National Archives, and a host of museums and historical societies gave generously of their time during the final push toward completion—rushing through last-minute orders; checking dates, names, and facts; and, in general, applauding our project enthusiastically. The credit lines are small repayment to so many hard-working people and contributing institutions; we can only add, once again, thanks ever so much for all your help.

A young Aldo Leopold as Forest Assistant and Chief of the Reconnaisance Party, Apache National Forest, Arizona, ca. 1911. Courtesy Forest History Society.

CHAPTER 1

An American Legacy

Imagine what the United States would be like without its great forests, without the tree-covered expanses of the Appalachians, the Sierra Nevada, the Cascades, and the Rocky Mountains. More than a century ago, a small but influential group of American artists, writers, scientists, and intellectuals found reason to fear that very possibility, and thereby sparked a lively and growing dialogue about the consequences of forest depletion. From those first debates sprang the conservation movement. In terms of federal involvement, conservationists achieved their greatest breakthrough in 1891 with the passage by Congress of the Forest Reserve Act. The act empowered the president, without further consent from Congress, to proclaim forest "reserves" on the nation's public lands. In 1907 the forest reserves were renamed the *national forests*. Thus had the United States committed itself to ensuring that the warnings of its conservation prophets did not in fact come to pass.

The national forests—as both a system and an idea—are therefore a century old. That in itself is sufficient reason to commemorate their establishment. So too, this volume seeks to interpret the significance of the national forests, once more to challenge the reader to consider what the United States would be like had the system not evolved. Even today, it is often argued that the national forests should be broken up and sold to their various constituent groups, among them mining, ranching, and logging interests. The federal government, its critics charge, is too inefficient to manage the forests properly.

From practically the moment of its founding, and well into the nineteenth century, the United States was indeed committed to trans-

Announcing the so-called history of the United States, a billboard outside the White Mountain National Forest, New Hampshire, ca. 1922, symbolizes the common frontier attitude that the federal government should deed all public lands to private ownership. Erroneously, the billboard declares that even the national forest is open to settlement, in effect, that forest-purchase laws passed after the Homestead Act of 1862 are nonetheless null and void. National Archives (95G-165954).

ferring the public lands to private owners large and small. Beginning in the 1850s, for example, nearly 180 million acres of government territory (equal to the states of California, Oregon, and Washington combined) was awarded to the western railroads to help offset the risks of laying new track in unsettled areas. In other words, the grants were intended to speed construction of the railroads, which, in turn, would populate the West. Millions of acres more passed free to settlers under the Homestead Act of 1862; here again, the object was to encourage the settlement of more distant western lands.

At least initially, the policy of selling or deeding the public lands to settlers and investors seemed to make perfect sense. After all, how else was the government to raise its operating capital and to spur the economy? The point is that the United States has already experimented — and boldly — with the concept of privatization. Yet what our forebears eventually discovered, and what many of us have since forgotten, was that the result of privatization was not always what the nation had expected or wanted. Especially during the last third of the nineteenth century, speculators swarmed over the public domain in what has come to be known as "the great barbecue" of natural resources. The abuses, both real and alleged, of this land rush finally convinced thinking Americans of the need for significant land-use reforms.

What, then, might take the place of wholesale privatization? What policy or policies might allow the nation to develop its natural resources

Asher B. Durand (1796-1886), *In the Woods*, 1855, Oil on canvas, 60¾ x 48.
Durand may have been the greatest of the Hudson River school painters. His depictions of the woods give them a temple-like dimension. This painting is the masterpiece of the genre and set the standard for the esthetic appreciation of the spiritual values of the forest wilderness. Courtesy of the Metropolitan Museum of Art; Gift in memory of Jonathan Sturgis by his children, 1895.

William R. Leigh, *Hunting Mountain Sheep*, oil on canvas, 24 x 36, 1912; courtesy of R. H. Richard.

Left:
William R. Leigh, *Panning Gold, Wyoming*, oil on canvas, 32¼ x 40, 1949; courtesy of Buffalo Bill Historical Center.

Right:
Frederic Remington, Impressionistic scene of birches and dense woods, oil on board, 16⅛ x 12; Buffalo Bill Historical Center, Gift of the Coe Foundation.

Below:
Albert Bierstadt, *Island Lake, Wind River Range, Wyoming*, oil on canvas, 26½ x 40½, 1861; Buffalo Bill Historical Center.

Thomas Moran, *The Mountain of the Holy Cross, Colorado*, 1876, chromolithograph; Buffalo Bill Historical Center.

and yet at the same time to ensure the protection of those resources for the use and betterment of the American people at large?

Among the solutions that evolved, the national forests stood apart. The idea did not please everyone, nor are the national forests today any less controversial. It would be unfortunate, however, if that side of the debate distracted attention from the achievement itself. Invariably, some-

Although often ignored, the esthetic (and many would argue spiritual) associations of the national forests are graphically symbolized in the Mountain of the Holy Cross, Holy Cross (now White River) National Forest, Colorado. Worshipers gather on neighboring Notch Mountain, 1932. National Archives (95G-273083).

one will always object to the management of the national forests, especially to how resources viewed as scarce can be equitably protected or distributed. But that should not distract us from the fact of the achievement. That there is something to argue about—indeed something still *worth* arguing about—is the point of the story that everyone can and should appreciate.

There is no question, however, that the national forests are major contributors to an American sense of place, to an identity with landscape that transcends economics for its own sake. The founders of the national forest idea—if not all of the system's later managers—were consistent in their advocacy for landscape esthetics. The forests not only should be functional; they should be beautiful as well. If the national forest idea has strayed anywhere from its historical roots and principles, perhaps it has strayed the most here, in the protection of a sense of place, even if, by law, the primary purpose of the system is the responsible and sustainable development of forest lands. Indeed no greater challenge may face the national forests as they enter their second century. Must the price of extraction, in every case, be the loss of natural beauty? The loss of biological diversity? Or can better ways and means be found to protect these other important values, which, no less than concern for the nation's timber, grasslands, and watersheds, evolved as an important cornerstone of the national forest idea?

In the footsteps of Lewis and Clark: Ranger Griffin and Forest Guard Cameron on fire-patrol duty, Mount Silcox, Cabinet (now Lolo) National Forest, Montana, 1909. Among its many suggestive themes, this widely distributed official photograph celebrates the forest ranger as the custodian of America's pioneer spirit. Thanks to the forests themselves, moreover, all Americans can recapture a sense of the Old West and, like Rangers Griffin and Cameron, imagine that they are lord and master over limitless horizons. National Archives (95G-59298).

Obviously, as long as such questions are being raised, the idea itself will be evolving. Evolving, then, into what? What indeed is the essential spirit of the national forest idea today? Is it enough to say that it is the spirit of give-and-take—trying, as far as possible, to accommodate everyone's outstanding claims to national forest lands? A common expression within the Forest Service goes something like this: If everyone is mad at me some of the time, then I must be doing my job, for if anyone is always satisfied, then I am probably giving that person too much. The knowledge that everyone is a bit dissatisfied is reassurance that no one is being favored.

Historically, the checklist began with timber, scenery, game animals, and watersheds but then, almost immediately, lengthened to include mining, grazing, irrigation, and hydropower generation. Fire protection also mushroomed into a major obligation, followed, after mid-century, by increasing demands for the recognition of all wilderness and wildlife values, as distinct from those basically restricted to sport hunting and fishing.

It is small wonder that the Forest Service has come to see itself as the Solomon of natural resources. But again, is judging between the legitimacy of competing interests what the forest *idea* is all about? Does the significance of the idea reside in some intangible quality evoking an American sense of place or rather (as some in the Forest Service have argued) in the politics and personalities of the management process itself?

To the historian, in either case, the spirit of an institution is the composite of its past. And that means its ideals, not just its laws and personalities. The spirit of the national forests, like that of the nation, lies somewhere in the collective consciousness of all who participate, not just those who manage.

The manager is tempted to accommodate new challenges by retooling past definitions. That may seem to work initially, yet it is the nature of anything spiritual to resist definition. The public will make up its own mind, and that "mind" is just as likely to be at odds with the consensus of management.

Probing the collective consciousness that is the American people as a whole, Aldo Leopold has probably come closest to the meaning of the national forests in the twentieth century. "I am glad I shall never be young without wild country to be young in," he wrote. "Of what avail are forty freedoms without a blank spot on the map?" He might have added: without a *green* spot on the map. A simple glance at a Rand McNally road atlas reveals broad bands of green, extending up and down the regional spines of the nation. They reassure, in an instant, that freedom of opportunity is still alive in the United States, whether someone seeks a new start that is spiritual or economic or even both.

Reconciling the spiritual and the economic is no easy task. In the liturgy of the Forest Service, it has met—and is meeting—that challenge successfully. Although implying no disparagement of the agency's motives, that liturgy can still be used to vindicate management decisions rather than to expedite the search for the *meaning* behind the process. The process is so important because we hope it never has to end. Like Aldo Leopold, the large majority of Americans still take comfort in the thought that the national forest system—as a working derivative of frontier America—has somehow guaranteed that the frontier will never leave us and, more specifically, that no amount of cultural dilution elsewhere will ever threaten our fundamental quest for new opportunities.

Can we indeed go on indefinitely? Will something of our frontier heritage always be with us? That all depends on our willingness to address the past honestly, to determine precisely what we have—and therefore what we stand to lose—with each new change of course affecting the public lands. One thing is certain: The history of conservation would have been very different without the national forests and the singular combination of opportunities the forests have come to represent. In this, their centennial year, that fact is worth examining anew, the better to understand the past—and more important—the present and the future of these very special lands.

At the head of Rattlesnake Creek in a remote drainage of the original Yellowstone Park Timber Land Reserve, the ranger's log cabin is barely visible at the right edge of the woods. Early rangers on the forest reserves and national forests patrolled vast areas on horseback or snowshoes and lived off the land while they surveyed, mapped, measured, and watched for poachers and fire. Photograph by Jack Richard, Cody, Wyoming.

--------- CHAPTER 2 ---------

The Origins of Conservation

Unquestionably, the protection of America's forests is an important esthetic issue. Yet in seeking out the origins of forest conservation, we understand why esthetics have generally been viewed as secondary to the fear of resource scarcity. Beginning in colonial times, the economy of the United States was dependent on the abundance of wood. Wood was the basic ingredient of every major industry, from shipbuilding in New England to ironworking in the forges of Pennsylvania. The plantations of the American South also relied on large quantities of wood to store and cure their products. By the middle of the nineteenth century, as the railroads came of age, the drain on forest products further accelerated. Wood was still the common fuel, and the belching steam engines burned enormous amounts to maintain their peak efficiency. No less vital were the wooden ties that bound the tracks in place. And still more wood was required for sidings, trestles, buildings, and rolling stock.

The problems of scarcity were first noticed around major centers of population. Indeed, hardly had the settlement of North America begun when spot shortages of timber appeared. Predictably, settlers were tempted to cut first the timber that was closest to home. Even at modest rates of cutting, only a few years elapsed before the nearest supplies were exhausted. Afterward, timber and fuel had to be imported over longer and longer distances. Consequently, by the end of the colonial period, Boston, New York, and Philadelphia, among other growing cities, were bringing in their fuel and building materials from many miles away.

The clearance of woodlands for agriculture also contributed to long-range timber scarcities. Led by its pioneers, the nation had set out to remake its forests into farms. In the initial stages of forest clearance, a few timber products might be sold. Even so, these were generally one-time sales, a temporary means of raising cash while the settler readied his fields for the plow. Otherwise, the forest was still considered an obstacle to agricultural prosperity. Although the wise farmer kept a few acres in trees for his own fuel and building needs, there was no lasting incentive, either cultural or economic, for him and his neighbors to manage their woodlands as a permanent cash crop.

In the prevailing climate of opinion that forests were superabundant, the first efforts at conservation were understandably haphazard and, for the most part, generally unsuccessful. As early as 1626, Plymouth Colony passed ordinances regulating the cutting and sale of timber on colony lands. Although it had been only six years since the landing of the *Mayflower* Pilgrims, the disappearance of timber closest to the settlements was already being noticed. The Pilgrims had moved quickly to head off the problem, possibly because of their knowledge of conditions back home in Europe, where timber shortages had become acute. As recent arrivals, the Pilgrims had witnessed Europe's problems firsthand. Accordingly, it was not inconceivable to them that North America itself could eventually suffer timber scarcities.

Thus the urge to conserve natural resources was strongest at the point of first encounter with North America, that is, where the concerns of the Old World had not yet been undermined by the seductive wealth of the New. In 1681, for example, William Penn, the proprietor of Pennsylvania, decreed that for every five acres his colonists cleared for settlement, one must be kept in forest. The basis of Penn's decree was his experience in England. After centuries of indiscriminate cutting, even the Royal Navy could no longer locate timbers large enough to build its biggest warships.

Like William Penn, the British government resolved to head off the problem in the forests of North America. If only for strategic needs, the best trees in the British colonies were to be protected from the axe. Consequently, ten years after Penn's decree, British authorities established the so-called broad arrow policy in royal lands across New England. The object was to protect the best stores of timber, principally white pine, for use as masts, spars, and hulls by the growing Royal Navy. Colonial officials reserved the trees desired for naval construction by marking them with a "broad arrow," so named because the hatchet strokes of the foresters suggested an arrowhead. But whatever the brand

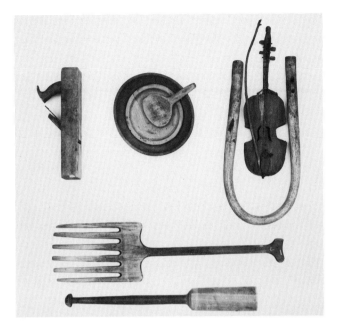

Americans of the 18th and 19th centuries, seeing apparently endless forests, became dependent upon wood not only for fuel and building materials but for many of the tools of living. The average American was also more conversant than Americans today in the variety of woods and their uses. The homemade fiddle, ox bow, kitchen servers, carpenter's plane, hayfork, and mallet are made of several woods, including maple, poplar, elm, and birch. Courtesy of Buffalo Bill Historical Center.

looked like, most colonists ignored it. Simply, the enforcement of the edict over such a wide area was highly impractical.

By the eighteenth century, a growing curiosity about the forest environment in both Europe and North America had partially offset the pioneer's indifference. Gradually, scientists, artists, and adventurers turned inward from the coastal settlements and, for the first time, began systematic studies of the continent's unique kaleidoscope of plants, birds, and animals. Among these pioneer naturalists, John James Audubon has long stood apart. Audubon's distinguished predecessors included Mark Catesby, Alexander Wilson, and John and William Bartram. A full century before Audubon started painting the birds of eastern North America, Mark Catesby had immersed himself in the natural history of Virginia and the Carolinas. By the close of the colonial period, the Bartrams had explored much of the territory between Florida and Pennsylvania, extending westward from the Atlantic Ocean into the Appalachian front. Audubon was further inspired by the paintings of Alexander Wilson and, like Wilson, sold purchase agreements, or subscriptions, to raise capital for his travels.

Thus were thousands of armchair explorers introduced to the forests of North America without ever leaving the comfort and security of their own homes. Granted, those early introductions were incomplete;

whatever their gifts as scientists and as artists, the naturalists had to appeal to the tastes of their benefactors and subscribers. The more popular the subject matter, the more likely it was to command advance payment. In any case, unless the naturalist's science could be sold as art, the science itself could not continue. That meant, in the long run, less attention to the composition of the forest environment as a whole. But it also meant, in compensation, a growing appreciation for the beauty and diversity of the natural world. As the historian Roderick Nash has noted, "The literary gentleman wielding a pen, not the pioneer with his axe, made the first gestures of resistance against the strong currents of antipathy." If the historical record is regrettably incomplete, ignoring much that has since vanished from the face of North America, it is also true that the natural sciences greatly benefited from their original availability, as art, to wealthy patrons of discovery both in America and abroad.

That very emphasis on esthetics—on the *beauty* of the natural world—was the second important cornerstone of American conserva-

Beginning with the early settlement of North America, pioneers eager to clear their land quickly resorted to girdling, a practice learned from the Indians. Girdling called for cutting entirely through the bark around the tree and leaving it to die standing; the leaves generally fell in a few weeks, allowing crops to take root in full sunlight. At best, the practice could be justified for saving time and labor; at worst, it epitomized the common American attitude that forests were superabundant. Shown here is a mountaineer's field along the Upper Tuckaseigee River, North Carolina, 1901. National Archives (95G-25421).

tion. Like the growing fear of resource scarcities, the appreciation of natural beauty gave Americans added incentive to consider the need for greater restraints on wasteful exploitation. All that remained for conservation to take hold in the public mind was a proper series of events to bridge the last remaining gap between indifference and concern.

In retrospect, the first important step in that process was the American Revolution. Suddenly, the young nation was on its own, torn apart, in effect, from the foundations of Western civilization. What, Americans asked, might take the place of their former linkages, as colonists of the British Empire, to European culture? Even more to the point, what symbols of cultural identity distinguished the United States in the family of nations? Who among America's artists, for example, compared to a Michelangelo or a Da Vinci? What great works of American architecture compared to the Parthenon or the Sistine Chapel? And who among America's authors might eventually be recognized as a Milton or a Shakespeare? In short, what tangible evidence—what *convincing* evidence—could Americans cite as proof of their claim that the United States deserved recognition for contributing to the advancement of world civilization?

Much to the dismay of anxious nationalists, there were few convincing answers. World-class literature, art, and architecture would be decades—even centuries—in the making. As late as 1820, the noted British critic Sydney Smith asked derisively, "In the four quarters of the globe, who reads an American book? or goes to an American play? or looks at an American picture or statue?" Smith's insulting tone aside, his point was still well-taken. In terms of cultural heritage, at least, the United States had yet to prove itself.

Gradually, nationalists turned to their last resort—the unique *promise* of America. If they could not find refuge in the past, they would escape to the future. Unlike Europe, their argument unfolded, the United States was not encumbered by a history of privilege and aristocracy. Granted, Europe had many enviable qualities, including great works of art and storied traditions. But regardless of that heritage, the potential of Europe had finally run its course. The future of Western civilization was on the American side of the Atlantic, where democracy had finally triumphed over monarchy and dictatorship. Nor was there any greater proof of America's eventual superiority than her unbounded wilderness, a vast storehouse of land and natural resources stretching another three thousand miles to the Pacific. Thus Philip Freneau, for example, a strident young nationalist writing at the dawn of American independence,

Karl Bodmer, *Forest Scene on the Lehigh, Pennsylvania*, ca. 1834, black and white aquatint, Buffalo Bill Historical Center.

looked westward to the Mississippi as the new "prince of rivers in comparison of whom the *Nile* is but a small rivulet, and the *Danube* a ditch."

Though obviously exaggerated, such claims formed the basis of a working national identity, a consciousness founded on the conviction that nature, if not culture, might serve as the enduring symbol of democracy's true resilience. And gradually, the nation's community of artists fully sensed the opportunity. Historically, the Grand Tour of Europe had established an artist's legitimacy. Although artists, writers, and intellectuals continued to make the Grand Tour, by the 1820s and 1830s many were also returning to the United States more committed than ever to portraying their own country's freshness and vitality. "In America," remarked Thomas Cole, for example, "all nature is new to art." Thus Cole set the theme for an entire generation of American landscape painters, the renowned Hudson River school. Granted, the United States offered none of the prized romantic scenes so commonplace in Europe—mountaintop castles, cathedral villages, ancient harbors, and storied battlefields. Instead, Cole challenged his colleagues to examine the mountains, rivers, forests, and seacoasts of New York and New England, where, despite random human interruptions, an even greater subject—the divinity of the universe as revealed through nature's mysteries—awaited the artist's brush.

The outcome could not have been foreseen at the time, but in turning to the natural world as their primary subject matter, the painters of the Hudson River school established esthetics—and not merely production—as one of the pillars of forest conservation. The Hudson River school corroborated what nationalists had been saying since independence—that America's distinctiveness was its wildness, a unique sense of place brought about principally by the absence of human works. Mountains, it followed, were security for both the artist and the nation's dwindling forests. Generally, settlement skirted the mountains; most pioneers lacked the technology—or the need—to probe deeply beyond the foothills or the fertile river valleys. Even in the Northeast, wild nature still abounded. All that was required of Cole and his contemporaries was to climb the highest promontory, to rise above civilization by scaling the distant peaks of the Catskills, the Adirondacks, or the White Mountains. Below, settlement might be portrayed as the normal course of events, eddying about the mountainsides but leaving the peaks—and their forests—largely intact. Nature on high, it was safe to assume, would always be nature in the wild. Thanks to mountains, neither the nation's cultural horizon nor the original forest that was one of that horizon's most distinctive traits would ever be fully circumscribed.

At least for the moment, any disquieting evidence to the contrary could be pushed into the background. Like forest clearings, towns, and settlements, the spreading influences of American industry were only faintly acknowledged. By the 1840s, for example, artists were confronted by the problem of the railroad in the landscape; at first, they portrayed the locomotives and cars far off in the distance, veiled by the mists of an intervening waterway or a summer day's haze. Perhaps somewhere against the horizon, the rising smoke of a locomotive further blended with the clouds, again as if to suggest that technology and nature had in fact become reconciled. But ultimately, even artistic license could hide only so much. Past the midpoint of the nineteenth century, the rapidity of industrial change in the northeastern landscape could no longer be distorted. The conventional wisdom of the Hudson River school—to paint accurately and without embellishment—was its artists' own undoing. Accuracy demanded that every change, however subtle, be truthfully recorded. Once the "machine" was in the "garden," so too the artist had to admit that the garden had been despoiled.

In the end, the pioneer's axe had triumphed. The pioneer had blazed the way, and industry had shortly followed. Everywhere, it seemed, the forest was coming down. With a considerable sense of shock and great foreboding, a few Americans had begun to question what all the change portended. How would the character of the nation be affected if its forests were all destroyed? Only a few decades earlier, the question had been irrelevant. Suddenly, perceptive people had come to realize that superabundance was a myth. Even the greatest and most bountiful nations might fall victim to the excesses of exploitation. For the United States, the loss would be doubly calamitous. Not only did the nation depend on wood for commerce and industry, but the United States had also taken intellectual and cultural refuge in the promise of an unspoiled continent.

Nature was culture. The more Americans altered the landscape, reducing both its freshness and its diversity, the less credibility could be given that reasoning.

Logging practices of the type that so alarmed George Perkins Marsh and other nineteenth-century activists continued well into the twentieth century, especially in the American South. This cabin near Hyden, Kentucky, photographed in September 1940, is in danger of being washed away should the skid road carrying logs to the left become a conduit for a flash flood. Photograph by Marion Post Wolcott, Library of Congress (LC-USF-34-55743-D).

Blount County, Tennessee, ca. 1933: This scene was repeated countless times from Maine to Georgia and west to the Mississippi Basin. Uncontrolled running water has stolen the fertility of this farm for years, and now the owners have abandoned it. Library of Congress (LC-USZ62-37468).

Finally, all of the necessary elements for conservation were firmly in place. In paintings and engravings, and across the landscape itself, the rudiments of awareness were more and more visible. Partly a response to fear and partly a response to appreciation, the first inklings of conservation had taken hold in the American mind. To be sure, the concept that the government should manage natural resources was still largely unformed. But in the evolution of concern lay the necessary prerequisite for suggesting this alternative. All that remained was for the seriousness of the problem to convince the public of the need. Meanwhile, the nation did not lack for prophets. Along different paths and sometimes for different reasons, American artists, writers, and nationalists had all been the founders of awareness. Conservation had taken its first and most important step.

A celebration of conquest: Loggers pose on a western red-cedar stump near Deming, Washington, ca. 1925. Parents, wives, and sweethearts probably received this picture in the form of a postcard prepared on-site by the photographer as proof to loved ones that life and limb were still intact in the ever dangerous woods. National Archives (95G-195968).

CHAPTER 3

Prophets and Precedents

In every movement there is a moment of convergence, a time when distinct but parallel concerns are finally brought together. For forest conservation, a likely candidate for the honor would be the year 1864. The man of the hour was George Perkins Marsh—diplomat, scientist, and Vermont politician. During the preceding two hundred years, explorers and naturalists, then artists and politicians, had discovered the symbolic linkages between landscape and culture. Even hunters and fishermen, sensing the decline in their prey, had begun calling for the protection of the nation's forests and streams. Without habitat, sportsmen had come to recognize, fish and wildlife could not survive. But all that was prelude. Needed was convergence, the translation of awareness into meaningful action. Conservation required leadership and greater unity of purpose. Above all, conservation needed the voice of a philosopher, someone to remind concerned artists, intellectuals, sportsmen, and politicians that whatever differences of opinion might continue to divide them, the protection of America's forests was in fact everyone's top priority.

In George Perkins Marsh, conservation found that thread of unity. Growing up in Woodstock, Vermont, he had learned important lessons about human degradation of the environment. With his father, a successful attorney, Marsh unraveled the complicated relationships between forest cover and streamflow. Every spring, it seemed that the river through Woodstock rapidly rose and spilled over its banks but then, as summer progressed, often dried up completely. Marsh and his father traced the source of the problem to lumbering and grazing in the mountains behind

Portrait of George
Perkins Marsh,
courtesy of Forest
History Society.

the town. Years later, as the U.S. minister to Turkey, Marsh recalled
these experiences in Vermont and applied them in his studies of the
eastern Mediterranean, arguing that its ancient civilizations had declined,
in large part, because deforestation and overgrazing had destroyed their
resource base.

His lifelong interest in European history, his mastery of European
languages, his distinguished political career, and his extensive travels
abroad—all these attributes (and more) uniquely fitted George Perkins
Marsh for unquestionably his greatest contribution, the publication in
1864 of his book *Man and Nature*. "Man is everywhere a disturbing
agent," he wrote, setting the theme of this classic study. "Wherever he
plants his foot, the harmonies of nature are turned to discords." *Man
and Nature* went on to describe, in exhaustive but absorbing detail, the
effects of human settlement on forests, water, wildlife, and deserts. Yet
forests were the key, and it was the prospect that the United States
might repeat the environmental mistakes of the ancients that concerned
Marsh the most. "We have now felled forest enough everywhere, in many

Thomas Cole, *View on the Catskill, Early Autumn*, oil on canvas, 39 x 63, 1837.
All of the elements of the eastern forest esthetic, as represented in the paintings of the Hudson River school, are beautifully depicted in this famous masterpiece. Courtesy of the Metropolitan Museum of Art. Gift in memory of Jonathan Sturges by his children, 1895.

Thomas Cole, *River in the Catskills*, 1843, oil on canvas, 28¼ x 41½
Only six years have passed, and note what has happened to Cole's picturesque river scene. The trees are now stumps, more fields have been cleared, and a railroad bridge and locomotive practically dominate the middle landscape. Only the distant mountains seem to have escaped the relentless march of progress. Courtesy of the Museum of Fine Arts, Boston. M. and M. Karolik Collection.

Jasper Francis Cropsey, *Starrucca Viaduct, Pennsylvania*, 1865, oil on canvas, 22½ x 36⅜, courtesy of the Toledo Museum of Art, Gift of Florence Scott Libbey.

districts far too much," he maintained. "Let us restore this one element of material life to its normal proportions, and devise means for maintaining the permanence of its relations to the fields, the meadows, and the pastures, to the rain and the dews of heaven, to the springs and rivulets with which it waters the earth." For indeed, he concluded, unless the nation heeded the warnings of past deforestations and maintained "an approximately fixed ratio between . . . woodland and plough land," its future as "a well-ordered and stable commonwealth" would also be in jeopardy.

In retrospect, *Man and Nature* aroused thoughtful Americans because its warnings were finally inescapable. The logging frontier had long since advanced across the breadth of New England, leaving but remnants of the original forest cover that Marsh had known as a boy. The second-growth forest taking hold would be a very different composition, especially deficient, for example, in large stands of white pine. Meanwhile, the search for white pine had extended to the forests of New York and Pennsylvania, and with their supplies soon exhausted,

John Fery, *Mount Hood, Oregon*, oil on canvas, courtesy of Boise Cascade.
Whether in the East or West, artists wrestled with the railroad in the American landscape. Up close, the railroad symbolized all of the power of industry to degrade the environment. Most artists, accordingly, preferred relegating trains to the background, although positioning them in the center of a painting was another way of subtly admitting that the railroad was the predominant influence on the countryside.

the logging frontier would be on the move yet again, crossing Ohio and Indiana before settling, for another assault, in Wisconsin, Michigan, and northern Minnesota. Such was the course of events that unfolded before Marsh's growing readership and that finally, after two hundred years of indifference to the fate of America's woodlands, shocked a few attentive Americans into endorsing his pleas for genuine reform.

Like any important sourcebook, *Man and Nature* was a unifying force, a crucible of knowledge for conservation's early champions. In that respect alone, its significance as a milestone on the road to the national forests cannot be overestimated. Although the first forest reserves would not be proclaimed for another quarter century, *Man and Nature* lent legitimacy to the emerging body of opinion that some of the public lands should be retained in government ownership, both state and federal. Noting the march of the logging industry into northern New York State, for example, Marsh himself called for the protection of the Adirondacks and other comparable areas, "as far as possible" in their "primitive condition." Only large tracts of land, he concluded, would effectively serve as an "asylum" for wildlife and as "a garden for the recreation of the lover of nature."

John James Audubon, *Barred Owl*, engraving on paper, 37½ x 27¾ and *American Bison or Buffalo*, 1845, colored lithograph, 19 x 25⅛, both Buffalo Bill Historical Center.

That Marsh included natural beauty among the reasons for protecting forests underscores again the influence of landscape esthetics on the conservation movement. For the most part, Marsh has been typecast as utilitarian, that is, as essentially concerned with the practical applications of forest, soil, and water conservation. Nonetheless, his concerns were obviously broader, and indeed his acknowledgment of the importance of natural beauty was to prove most prophetic. For in fact, the first significant shift in federal policy with regard to the western public lands led to the establishment of the national parks years before the national forests. The year Marsh published *Man and Nature* — specifically, on June 30, 1864 — President Abraham Lincoln signed legislation granting Yosemite Valley and the Mariposa Grove of giant sequoias to the state of California "for public use, resort, and recreation," to be held "inalienable for all time." Eight years later, on March 1, 1872, President Ulysses S. Grant signed legislation establishing a great "public park" around the geyser basins, canyons, and lakes of the fabled Yellowstone wilderness, but Grant, unlike Lincoln, did not transfer management of the area to another government jurisdiction. Thus Yellowstone, rather than Yosemite, was the first government preserve to be called a national park. More important, however, was the principle that both Yosemite and Yellowstone had firmly established. When public lands of national significance were visibly threatened by exploitation, the government had the right — indeed the duty — to maintain those lands for public benefit.

Once again, these esthetic foundations for forest conservation have been largely discounted. True enough, there were other important precedents that were strictly utilitarian in nature, among them legislation passed as early as 1817 for the protection of live oak and red cedar reserves by the U.S. Navy. Federal legislation in 1827 and 1831 further strengthened the sanctions against cutting both species on all reserved lands. But like the broad arrow policy of the British colonial government, these sanctions were intended to protect specific trees, not entire forests. The protection of all-encompassing expanses of the nation's public lands did in fact await the establishment of national parks. At nearly thirty-five hundred square miles in area, Yellowstone in particular anticipated the desirable limits of a true working forest. But without that first crucial step — the consensus that large government set-asides were indeed in the public interest — the national forests themselves could never have been realized.

At least initially, any distinctions between the esthetic and the practical applications of forests were consistently blurred. In 1875, for example, botanists, landscape gardeners, and estate owners formed the American Forestry Association and, in advocating forest conservation, stressed not only the functional principles espoused in *Man and Nature* but also the natural beauty of trees. In 1876, concerned New England-ers, many from the Boston area, founded the Appalachian Mountain Club. Like the American Forestry Association, the Appalachian Mountain Club decried both the waste of forest resources and the loss of natural beauty. Gradually, the organizations diverged, with the American Forestry Association devoting more and more attention to the importance of forests as watersheds and perpetual sources of timber. But the precedent had been set. Whatever differences of opinion later characterized the movement, forest conservation began in the public mind as a stirring of conscience, an indivisible bond between trees as a commercial resource and a common national heritage. The latter principle might be ignored, but not without touching a wellspring of indignation as deep as the nation's search for a distinctive national identity. Ultimately, the public would not support conservation without a conscience, a conscience defined as the recognition of true equality between the needs of national production and the integrity of the forest environment as a source of literary, scientific, and artistic inspiration.

Wherever forest conservation took hold, the esthetic and the practical went hand in hand. And so it remained as the Middle West also weighed the need for greater foresight, largely at the urging of Julius Sterling Morton, a Nebraska farmer, newspaper editor, and crusading politician. In Morton's estimation, the planting and cultivation of orchards, ornamental flowers, and special shrubs would break up the so-called monotony of the state's prairies and plains. The Nebraska State Horticultural Society agreed and on January 4, 1872, heard Morton further proclaim orchards as "missionaries of culture and refinement." He added that orchards, "together with a few forest trees," would transform Nebraska both "mentally and morally" into "the best agricultural state." The State Board of Agriculture immediately adopted his resolution designating April 10, 1872, as Arbor Day, "set apart and consecrated for tree planting in the state of Nebraska." By 1874 Arbor Day had been recognized as an annual observance, and by 1882 five additional states—Kansas, Minnesota, North Dakota, Tennessee, and Ohio—had joined with Nebraska in promoting the event.

For those unmoved by esthetics, however practical in application, tragedy still acted as a motivating force for conservation. And no tragedy equalled the infamous Peshtigo Fire. On the night of October 8 and

Political cartoon, signed "Rehse," pen and ink on paper, 18 x 21.
Congressional efforts to limit the national forests are lampooned in this 1909 cartoon. The national forests have always been subject to wider use than any other parts of the public domain. Competition for the forest resources—whether timber, minerals, water, range, or recreation—has often resulted in intense political pressure from all quarters. Courtesy of the USDA Forest Service, Grey Towers National Historic Landmark.

Future Generation: Did All This Happen Within Your Time, Grandpa?
Present Generation: Yes, My Boy.
Future Generation: What Did You Let 'Em Do It For?

into the morning of October 9, 1871, the lumbering town of Peshtigo, Wisconsin, was battered by a "hurricane of flame." Within hours, the entire town, its environs, and nearly 1.3 million acres of land had been swept by a wall of fire so devastating and so intense that the term *fire storm* is believed to have originated in later accounts of the event. The human toll was equally frightening—at least fifteen hundred lives, many lost as people tried to flee the raging inferno. But flight was literally hopeless as the fire, fueled by months of lingering drought and the awesome winds generated by its own blazing heat, overtook everything in its path.

Although months passed before accounts of the Peshtigo Fire were fully compiled, no other incident offered more somber and convincing proof of the warnings of George Perkins Marsh. Nor is it surprising that in the aftermath of Peshtigo and similar maelstroms of destruction, the nation's commitment to forest conservation markedly increased. Certainly by the early 1880s, calls for the protection of America's forests were anything but new. In government, for example, Carl Schurz, the secretary of the interior, was among those who added forcefully to the warnings of *Man and Nature*. "Nowhere is a wasteful destruction of the forests fraught with more dangerous results than in mountainous regions," he reported at the beginning of his term of office in 1877. "The timber grows mostly on the mountain sides, and when these mountain sides are once stripped bare, the rain will soon wash all the earth necessary for the growth of trees from the slopes down into the valleys, and the renewal of the forests will be rendered impossible forever." The aversion of "such evil results" called for swift "remedial measures," especially prohibitions against the sale and settlement of "all timber-lands still belonging to the United States." In addition, "government agents should be provided to protect the timber on public lands from degradation." He concluded, "I am so deeply impressed with the importance of this subject that I venture to predict, the Congress making efficient laws for the preservation of our forests will be ranked by future generations in this country among its greatest benefactors."

Like George Perkins Marsh, Carl Schurz relied heavily on his prior experience and training abroad. A native of Germany, he also had first-

A plow stands as mute testimony to decades of thoughtless waste in Jackson County, Alabama, April 1937. From deforestation and overcultivation have sprung the final insult to the land—erosion. Undoubtedly the farmer has moved on, abandoning his plow but probably not his ignorance. Photo by Arthur Rothstein, Library of Congress (LC-USF34-25438-D).

hand knowledge about the consequences of forest depletion in Europe, as well as the continent's turn to modern forestry to alleviate the problem. That is, at least some countries had responded, and Germany was among the leaders. Indeed, another German immigrant, Bernhard Eduard Fernow, arrived in the United States in 1876 and would also play a significant role in the evolution of American forestry. The point again is that before any of these prophets of conservation could be truly effective, the United States had to be convinced that its forests were indeed in serious jeopardy. In that respect, the Peshtigo Fire, for example, served far more effectively as a national call to arms than even the most strident warnings of Marsh and his followers.

The larger problem, it was agreed, was that the frontier was rapidly retreating and, by the 1880s, survived only in pockets of the American West. However large, those pockets in no way compared to the original frontier, when everything west of the Mississippi had seemed ripe for the taking. At the very least, the problem of the vanishing frontier called out for further study, and the nation's forests, it was evident,

In the wake of the pioneers came new logging technologies, most notably steam-driven machinery and the narrow-gauge railroad. Even the steepest mountain slopes were no longer off-limits to exploitation. Shown here is railroad-based logging in the Great Smoky Mountains of Tennessee, 1913. National Archives (95G-15511-A).

Charles Sprague Sargent portrait, courtesy of the Library of Congress.

should be part of that endeavor. In a preliminary study, John Wesley Powell distinguished between the humid East and the arid West, noting that annual rainfall across the so-called Arid Region was well below the twenty inches needed to sustain agriculture without irrigation. In any case, both the irrigable lands and the timberlands constituted "but a small fraction of the Arid Region." Conservation, it followed, was mandatory for settlement, especially if the lands suitable for farming, but lacking in water, were to be brought under cultivation. "Here, individual farmers, being poor men, cannot undertake the task," Powell concluded. The solution was a program of federal conservation, beginning with the passage by Congress of "carefully considered legislation."

Powell, a geologist (famed as the first explorer to traverse the length of the Colorado River through the Grand Canyon in 1869), thought of forests as watersheds to sustain reclamation. But although Congress was willing to listen, and in 1878 published his *Report on the Lands of the Arid Region of the United States* as a government document, little came of his basic ideas until the turn of the century. His immediate contributions were scientific and philosophical, anticipating again, above all, the need for a comprehensive program of national conservation.

That too was the principal message of Charles Sprague Sargent's *Report on the Forests of North America, Exclusive of Mexico*, sponsored in 1880 by the U.S. Bureau of the Census and published as a separate volume of the bureau's final analysis in 1883. "The forest wealth of the country is still undoubtedly enormous," Sargent maintained, reassuring government officials that their indifference to date had not been catastrophic. "Great as it is, however, it is not inexhaustible, and the forests of the United States, in spite of their extent, variety, and richness . . . cannot always continue productive if the simplest laws of nature governing their growth are totally disregarded." In Sargent's estimation, for example, fire and overgrazing inflicted "greater permanent injury upon the forests of the country than the ax." More than regulations against logging, as "recklessly and wastefully" as the axe was generally applied, would be required to save the nation's forests from irreversible harm.

In Sargent, the ideas of George Perkins Marsh had once more come full circle. It was in fact a reading of *Man and Nature* that had sparked Sargent's early interests in conservation and horticulture. A graduate of Harvard University, he was appointed director of its botanic garden in 1873 and later became director of the Arnold Arboretum at Jamaica Plain, Massachusetts. In 1883, coinciding with the publication of his *Report on the Forests of North America*, he actively joined in the effort to persuade the New York state legislature to enact legislation for the protection of the Adirondacks. Barely twenty-five hundred square miles of the original Adirondack wilderness still survived, he reported, and even that remnant was under siege by armies of reckless loggers, speculators, squatters, and hunters, all made more deadly by carelessness "in their smoking" and their "neglect to watch and properly extinguish the fires lighted for camp and cooking purposes."

Ultimately, the accelerating pace of destruction forced the state's hand. The *New York Times*, the *Nation*, and many other leading journals joined Sargent and his colleagues in attacking each delay. Support also continued to build from the state's urban community. As more and more trees were cut, cities and towns across upstate New York expressed alarm about the survival of the Adirondacks as a source of fresh water. And would the loss of critical watersheds also contribute to destructive levels of fluctuation in the state's waterways and canals? Via the Hudson River, which took its rise in the Adirondacks, even distant New York City was obviously dependent on the protection of the region.

Here, in retrospect, was the most important argument for conserving the forests of the Adirondacks. To be sure, there was concern for the forest itself and for the natural beauty of the Adirondacks. But conservation of the region had come to stand for something more, namely, the protection of public health. Politicians might quibble forever about the need to save trees, but they could hardly oppose—or delay indefinitely—measures to ensure the safety and security of their constituents. Forests, watersheds, natural beauty, and public health—all, especially the latter, formed an unbeatable combination for the final approval in 1885 of the Adirondack Forest Preserve.

Granted, like any new experiment, the preserve was more important for setting a precedent than for meeting its stated objectives. In truth, the Adirondack Forest Preserve would be decades in the making. The large majority of its original holdings had already been stripped of trees and then abandoned. In short, New York State had taken advantage of a common frontier practice—the principle of "cut and run." Of the approximately 681,000 acres that composed the original reserve, most had simply reverted to government ownership as a penalty for unpaid taxes. Theoretically, from those abandoned and denuded lands would rise a healthy new growth, which, in coming years, would develop into another mature forest. Only next time the forest would be carefully managed by state officials. At least that was the hoped-for result as New York State began the acquisition and consolidation of its new forest properties.

In the meantime, the Adirondack Forest Preserve was a most important precedent on the road to the national forests. If a major state could become actively involved in conservation efforts, it only stood to reason that the federal government should be doing more as well. So far, most of its contribution had been restricted to special reports and western field studies. Yet another fact-finding agency was the Division of Forestry, established in 1881 in the Department of Agriculture. But again, the division's lack of authority to *protect* forests was painfully obvious. All of the public lands were still under the control of the General Land Office in the Department of the Interior. The Division of Forestry, in other words, could do little more than suggest needed reforms. And clearly the most pressing reform was that being called for by Carl Schurz, John Wesley Powell, Charles S. Sargent, and their growing ranks of supporters, namely, that any forest lands remaining in federal ownership should be permanently closed to both settlement and corporate entry.

Irving R. Bacon, *The Life I Love*, 1902
So-called gentlemen of the chase, such as the obviously wealthy hunters depicted in Irving Bacon's graphic painting, founded the Boone and Crockett Club in 1887 to preserve the rules and spirit of sport hunting. It is said that the club made important behind-the-scenes contributions to the passage of the Forest Reserve Act of 1891. Buffalo Bill Historical Center.

The division's first chief, Franklin B. Hough, now worked closely with the scientific community to advance that agenda. The origins of his own four-volume study *Report upon Forestry* could be traced back to 1873 and the annual meeting of the American Association for the Advancement of Science, where Hough urged Congress and the states to begin enacting legislation on behalf of forest preservation. The AAAS endorsed his remarks and further petitioned Congress for the establishment of a commission to investigate the issue. Finally, in 1876, Congress appropriated two thousand dollars for a report under the auspices of the Department of Agriculture. That authorization in turn led to Hough's *Report upon Forestry* and largely to the realization of the Division of Forestry, established five years later.

Live oaks, Birabent Canyon, Los Padres National Forest, California; photograph by David Muench.

Santa Ynez Range,
Los Padres National
Forest, California;
photograph by
David Muench.

Snake River, Hells
Canyon, Oregon-
Idaho; photograph by
David Muench.

Mt. Magazine, Quachita National Forest, Arkansas; photograph by David Muench.

Tideland Marsh, Cedar Point, Croatan National Forest, North Carolina; photograph by David Muench.

Saguaro and volcanic arch, Superstition Wilderness, Tonto National Forest, Arizona; photograph by David Muench.

Ellowa Falls, Columbia River Gorge, Oregon; photograph by David Muench.

Dogwood blossoms, Hoosier National Forest, Indiana; photograph by David Muench.

Fern hammock spring, Ocala National Forest, Florida; photograph by David Muench.

Fern spread and hardwoods, Allegheny National Forest, Pennsylvania; photograph by David Muench.

As the chief of the division until 1883, Hough continued to press the case for the protection and management of all government-owned forests. His immediate successor was undistinguished, but in 1886 President Grover Cleveland appointed Bernhard E. Fernow to head the division. Like Hough, Fernow believed in a strong policy of government intervention in the nation's public lands. Toward that end, he immediately assembled a qualified research staff and underscored Hough's earlier recommendations for tree planting, experiment stations, and public education, to coincide with a program leading to the retention, in perpetuity, of the government's remaining forest areas.

One final bit of news piqued the nation's concern about the future of its forests. As part of the census of 1890, the government reported the closing of the American frontier. No longer was it possible to distinguish a clearly defined boundary between the settled and the unsettled halves of the country. The West, like the East, had been all but fully tamed. True, large islands of uninhabited territory remained in the region, but those islands were just that—fragments of the former whole. That seemingly inexhaustible supply of land—that once boundless storehouse of natural resources stretching all the way to the Pacific Ocean—had finally been settled and spoken for.

To say the least, thinking Americans were dismayed. Somehow the frontier had distinguished the United States from all other nations. Thanks to the presence of a frontier, America had a ready-made excuse for its lack of cultural achievements. Americans were too busy, too pre-occupied with building a country, to worry about the past. Art would come, and recognition too. But for now, the United States preferred retesting and renewing the strengths it had gained from centuries of confrontation with the North American wilderness. Suddenly, all that had changed. For the first time in its history, the United States would also have to learn to live within its means.

In retrospect, the United States had not run out of natural resources; new frontiers of extraction, from oil and natural gas to coal and uranium, awaited exploitation. Even so, the traditional frontier had been vitally important, and the knowledge of its passing seemed to hem the nation in, suggesting that those other latent possibilities—however large and unrealized—would never be quite the same.

Especially when it came to forests, the warnings of the past quarter century seemed finally to have been vindicated. It was time, critics repeated, to dust off the nation's land laws and look seriously into the future. The Yellowstone Park Act of 1872 offered a suggestive possibility. Congress took the cue and on October 1, 1890, set aside more than fifteen hundred square miles of the Sierra Nevada wilderness "as reserved forest lands." But a few days earlier, on September 25, "a public park" to protect the giant sequoias of the Sierra Nevada had also been approved. The act of October 1, 1890, "to set apart certain tracts of land in the State of California as forest reservations," further enlarged that "public park."

Today, the "park" is known as Sequoia National Park, and the "reserved forest lands" as Yosemite National Park. Clearly, the sponsors of the legislation had learned to take full advantage of the Yellowstone precedent. Led by the Southern Pacific Railroad, California's major land-holder, irrigationists in the San Joaquin Valley were eager to prevent the deforestation of neighboring mountain watersheds in the Sierra Nevada.

Fearing the decimation of native wildlife, sport hunters were among the earliest advocates for the establishment of national forests, which, it was hoped, would serve as breeding grounds for big game and as refuges from illegal poaching. The contradictory urge to exploit wildlife for commercial profit is underscored in this 1930 photograph of a trapper in the Tongass National Forest, Alaska. The skins fronting his cabin door are Alaskan brown bear. National Archives (95G-253711).

Terminology was less important than substantive results. Shrewdly, the irrigationists and the preservationists came together, wrapping one another's goals in the rhetoric of the other. Parks could be forests and forests could be parks. What difference did it make, as long as the Sierra Nevada and its watersheds could be protected from destruction?

As the nation stood on the eve of organized conservation, it seemed willing to take the best of both the functional and the esthetic, to mold the needs of each to the full advantage of the other. To reemphasize, if that commitment has since been lost, it did indeed exist—and flourish—during the founding years of conservation. Thus pushed into the forefront of the nation's consciousness, forest conservation had arrived at that critical stage of public and political awareness. Looking back to mid-century, the nation could readily assess the costs of its historical indifference. Similarly, while noting those changes across the land, the announced close of the frontier pointed to an uncertain future. One thing was now evident—what forests the United States already possessed were all it would ever possess. To be sure, some of those forests were expansive and still largely untouched. But given the fact that even larger forests had already fallen to the axe, could anyone take real comfort in the knowledge that so much remained?

The answer came swiftly. On March 3, 1891, Congress approved the Forest Reserve Act. Only a few years earlier, similar proposals had gotten nowhere, and indeed, the Forest Reserve Act itself has long been interpreted as an accident, the beneficiary of Congress's rush to complete its business in the waning hours of its closing session. Simply, the omnibus bill containing the forest reserve clause was not carefully read by everyone present. Had it been, more members would undoubtedly have objected to the provision allowing the president of the United States, without further consent from Congress, to proclaim forest reserves anywhere on the public domain. In short, the president had unilateral authority to circumvent the objections of any special interests, including the opponents of conservation in the legislative branch.

And President Benjamin Harrison did not waste any time in getting down to business. Just three weeks later, on March 30, 1891, he proclaimed the first of fifteen forest reserves established during his administration—the Yellowstone Park Timber Land Reserve, lying immediately to the east and southeast of the national park proper. From George Perkins Marsh to Bernhard Eduard Fernow, the prophets of conservation had finally been vindicated. There would indeed be public forests. Not everything in the country would fall blindly and completely to the axe.

Abraham Archibald Anderson, the first superintendent of the Yellowstone Park Timber Land Reserve, was an accomplished artist and architect, a friend of Theodore Roosevelt, the haughty scion of one of New York's first families, and the scourge of sheepmen who would overgraze the forest rangeland. Photograph by Charles J. Belden.

CHAPTER 4

Proclaiming a Heritage

Left to presidential discretion, the enlargement of the national forest system depended on the boldness and initiative of the man who occupied the White House. By the close of his administration in 1893, Benjamin Harrison had set aside 17,564,800 acres of forest reserves, an area nearly eight times the size of Yellowstone National Park. It was a dramatic and significant beginning, considering that Yellowstone had stood for eighteen years as the largest conservation project of any kind in the West. Other historians have noted the symbolism of the fact that the formal establishment of both national parks and national forests began in the greater Yellowstone area. But one important distinction remained: only Congress could establish a national park, whereas a national forest required nothing more than a presidential proclamation.

Despite growing opposition from a variety of western interests, Grover Cleveland added 22,420,860 acres to the forest reserve system, all just days before leaving office in March 1897. His successor, William McKinley, was considerably more conservative, protecting only 7,205,729 acres before his assassination in September 1901. Suddenly, Theodore Roosevelt was chief executive. Although the circumstances of his ascendancy were tragic and unexpected, in Roosevelt the nation had inherited a rare combination of talent, enthusiasm, and commitment to leadership. The conservation movement especially was energized and revolutionized. Earlier as governor of New York, and now as president, Roosevelt embraced conservation as the key to national health and prosperity. It was a period unlike any other in conservation history. It was, in many respects, conservation's Golden Age.

Predictably, Roosevelt attracted other dynamic individuals into government service, including his chief advisor on conservation matters, Gifford Pinchot. An astute administrator, Pinchot further shared with Theodore Roosevelt a background of family wealth and social influence. After his graduation from Yale University in 1889, Pinchot had sailed to Europe to study professional forestry. A year later he was back home, convinced that western Europe was decades ahead of the United States in the management and protection of its remaining forest lands.

On the strength of his knowledge, family connections, and outgoing personality, Pinchot's reputation quickly grew. In 1892 he was retained by Cornelius Vanderbilt to manage the Biltmore estate, the railroad tycoon's mansion and forest acreage near Asheville, North Carolina. Applying his recent training in sustained-yield forestry, Pinchot worked to turn the woodlands of the estate into a paying commercial asset. Confident that he had succeeded, in 1893 he opened an office in New York City as a private consulting forester.

More opportunities, assignments, and publicity came his way, among them an invitation to serve on the National Forestry Commission of the National Academy of Sciences. In 1896, charged with recommending management policies for the forest reserves, the commission toured the West. As he would do throughout his life, Pinchot urged the adoption of "practical" measures, above all, administering the public lands of the West as a perpetual storehouse of timber and water. Gradually, the concerns of livestock, mining, and power interests also advanced to the forefront of his thinking. In all instances, the key word was *use*. "The first duty of the human race," he later remarked in this vein, "is to control the earth it lives upon." Thus he took it upon himself, both officially and unofficially, to reassure the growing ranks of suspicious westerners that the forest reserves were indeed meant to be used and not simply to be protected.

That message was a popular one, and in 1898 Pinchot was chosen to head the Division of Forestry in the Department of Agriculture. Like his predecessors, he quickly came to resent the irony of the fact that the forests themselves were controlled by the General Land Office in the Department of the Interior. As he put it, he was "a forester without forests." No one directly affected by that situation, Pinchot included, had any intentions of standing idly by. Even before his appointment, the Forest Management Act of 1897 had specified that the forest reserves, regardless of which department actually controlled the acreage, were in fact intended for production and not strictly for preservation. It was all

Above:
Time and again throughout his career, Gifford Pinchot described the meticulous appearance of European forests to reassure outspoken critics that logging need not be destructive. This self-portrait, taken in Germany in 1889, shows Pinchot, unidentified children, and a grove of European larch. National Archives (95G-1158).

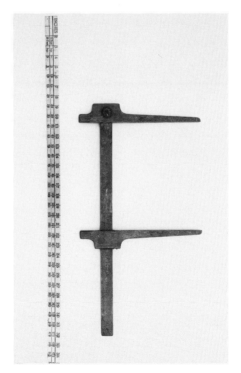

Right:
Gifford Pinchot's log rule and caliper are both well-used. Pinchot prided himself on his mastery of practical forestry, a profession he honed as the forester for the Vanderbilt's Biltmore estate in North Carolina. Courtesy of the USDA Forest Service, Grey Towers National Historic Landmark.

A great partnership in conservation: President Theodore Roosevelt and Gifford Pinchot discuss their many projects on a trip taken by the Inland Waterways Commission down the Mississippi River, October 1907. U.S. Forest Service photo, Library of Congress.

Pinchot might have wished, but he was still determined to wrest the forests proper from the Department of the Interior. With his agenda thus established, he worked tirelessly to see it through, bending the ear of the president, the Congress, or the American public about the absurdity of establishing forest reserves without a blueprint for their total management.

Other than *use*, the key term was *efficiency*. Ideally, resource "professionals"—foresters, hydrologists, geologists, and range scientists— would determine the proper and most efficient levels of resource consumption. In a scientifically managed forest, for example, mature trees would be cut while the younger growth was protected, assuring the eventual maturity of another forest "crop." Similarly, the forest would be guarded against fires and disease. In other words, there was more to managing a forest than just cutting wood. The cycles of growth and har-

Sanford Robinson Gifford (1823–1880), *Camping for the Night on Mansfield Mountain* c. 1868, Oil on canvas, 10 x 17. Gifford Pinchot's father was friend and patron to several of New York's leading artists. In fact, Gifford was named for Sanford Gifford who sold this painting to the Pinchot family in 1868. An esthetic appreciation of the woodland landscape, as well as a practical appreciation for the forest, were central to Pinchot's upbringing. In this picture, despite its apparently barren campsite, Gifford has suffused the wilderness with a romantic and calming glow. Courtesy of the Adirondack Museum, Blue Mountain Lake, N.Y.

vest, the best methods for controlling fire and insects, indeed the overall relationship of the trees to the total environment—all these things and more required the knowledge and training of experienced scientists. The United States would never run out of timber, waterpower, rangelands, and wildlife provided that each was systematically and efficiently handled on a sustained-yield basis.

Pinchot's challenge, it followed, was to convince the American people that their historical allowances of self-determination in the exploitation of natural resources now had to give way to the opinion of government "experts." Put another way, conservation was to be imposed on the population at large. That Pinchot succeeded was testimony not only to his initiative but also to his talent for building alliances with other like-minded civil servants. In hydrology, for example, W. J. McGee lent distinguished support to the broadening goals of federal conservation;

John F. Kensett, *Bergen Park, Colorado*, 1870, oil on canvas, 9¼ x 18½; Buffalo Bill Historical Center.
In art, if not in life, it is the classical American landscape that emotionally reigns supreme.

Above:
Carl Rungius, *In the Foothills*, oil on canvas, 30¼ x 40¼. Buffalo Bill Historical Center; gift of Mr. and Mrs. Larry Sheerin.

Opposite page:
Homer Dodge Martin (1836–1897), Untitled: Adirondack woodland n.d., oil on canvas, 16 x 24.
Martin flourished with the second generation of America's Hudson River school landscape painters. He was an outdoorsman with a love of the woods and a yen for solitude. This picture adopts many of the principles found in the woodland paintings of artists such as Asher B. Durand. Martin and other artists contributed esthetic ammunition to the scientific arguments for creation of the Adirondack Forest Preserve in 1885. Courtesy of the Adirondack Museum, Blue Mountain Lake, N.Y.

so too, Frederick H. Newell, as the director of the Reclamation Service (established in 1902), promoted major public works projects in flood control, irrigation, and the protection of vital watersheds. Collectively, Pinchot and his allies voiced a conviction as old as George Perkins Marsh—that *without* government intervention, the nation's forests, soils, and waterways would eventually be destroyed.

On February 1, 1905, President Theodore Roosevelt presented his chief advisor with the greatest victory of Pinchot's career. The 65 million acres of forest reserves already in existence were to be transferred from the Department of the Interior and placed under the care of Pinchot's Bureau of Forestry (formerly the Division of Forestry) in the Department of Agriculture. Barely another month later, Congress doubled the bureau's appropriation for the next fiscal year and further recognized its new title, the U.S. Forest Service.

As expected, Pinchot retained the honor of heading the agency. Still central to his philosophy was the conviction that proper management called for use. Wise use, more specifically, was the standard by which conservation as a whole would ultimately be judged as a success or as a failure. Pinchot, at least, had been handed every opportunity to mold the evolution of the conservation movement for years and years to come.

As his critics would later note, Pinchot's ideas were hardly new. He borrowed freely from his predecessors, even if, in later years, he failed to acknowledge their contributions. Undeniably, however, he made distinctive contributions of his own, not the least of which was his constant importuning of the president to withdraw additional forest lands by executive proclamation. The 65 million acres of forest reserves extant in February 1905 were but a fraction of the territory that should be added to the system, according to Pinchot. Simply, the president must do more.

Initially, Theodore Roosevelt had been cautious; throughout three previous administrations, the custom had been to add modestly to the forest system, at least until the eve of one's departure from office. Now in his second term, and with the Forest Service firmly established, Roosevelt agreed—it was time to throw caution to the winds. Over the next four years, he would add another 86 million acres to the forest reserve system, exceeding his own first-term total by nearly fivefold. At 151 million acres in 1909, the system was more than three times larger than when Roosevelt had taken office.

It was, indeed, an unprecedented achievement, but it had not been accomplished without the opposition from Congress that Roosevelt had feared. In 1907, chafing under his initiative, Congress finally moved to prohibit the president from proclaiming new forest reserves in six west-

Opposite page:
W. Herbert Dunton, *The Forest Ranger* (detail): oil on canvas, 32 x 22; courtesy of Mr. and Mrs. Kenn S. George.

ern states, coincidentally those states with the most forest acreage. As part of a major legislative package, the bill was too important for Roosevelt to simply veto it. Approve the restriction he must, but he knew he did not have to sign the bill *immediately*. The Constitution allowed him ten days, and he intended to use that time to good advantage. Over the next week and a half, the lights at the White House burned far into the night. Gifford Pinchot pored over his maps that indicated which forests still required protection in the six affected states. Each time Pinchot pointed his finger, Roosevelt drew his pen. By March 2, 1907, and the close of congressional business, more than 16 million acres of new forest reserves (known ever since as the "midnight forests") had been established, each reserve in direct opposition to the bill still sitting on Roosevelt's desk. Only when those forests had been safely proclaimed did the president finally sign the legislation, and by then, of course, he only took away his power to do what he had already done!

Below and opposite page:
Three maps showing the evolution of the national forest system, 1891–present. Courtesy of the Forest History Society.

National Forest System

1898: The forest reserves (national forests) created by Presidents Benjamin Harrison and Grover Cleveland. In this year, Gifford Pinchot became chief of the Division of Forestry (Forest Service).

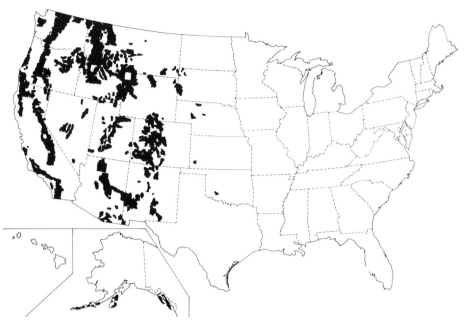

1907: Greatly expanded national forest system due to proclamations by President Theodore Roosevelt under the Forest Reserve Act of 1897.

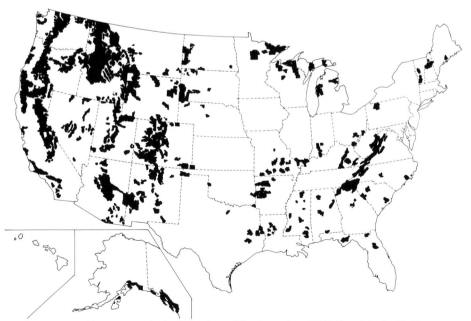

1980: The national forest system in the West shows little change from 1907. Forests in the East have been purchased since 1911 under the Weeks Act.

The officers of the Shoshone National Forest in 1907 reflect a variety of backgrounds and skills, from ranger Frank Sparhawk on the left, a former wrangler and lawman, to the professional forest supervisor, Harry Thurston, on the right. Photograph by F. J. Hiscock.

No greater challenge faced early rangers than determining the exact boundaries of Forest Service holdings. Until each boundary had been surveyed and marked, disputes with cattle ranchers, shepherds, and other landholders were almost certain to arise. This new boundary post along the government road west of Cody, Wyoming, March 1912, informs travelers of their arrival in the Shoshone National Forest. National Archives (95G-10762A).

Political cartoon, signed "Ding," pen and ink on paper, 29⅜ x 16½.
This famous cartoon by J. N. "Ding" Darling was published as President Theodore Roosevelt oversaw transfer of the forest reserves from the Interior Department to the Department of Agriculture where they could at last be administered by Gifford Pinchot and the Forest Service. Darling was an outdoorsman and conservationist who helped create the federal duck stamp program. Courtesy of the USDA Forest Service, Grey Towers National Historic Landmark.

Despite various boundary changes, consolidations, land exchanges, and other housekeeping chores, the national forest system today remains essentially as it was when Theodore Roosevelt left the White House. That is, in the *West* it is essentially the same; with but few exceptions,

A forest officer familiarizes himself with the Harney (now Black Hills) National Forest, South Dakota, from the top of Harney Peak, August 1911. National Archives (95G-385A).

the system in the East did not get under way until 1911. Under terms of the Weeks Act, Congress allowed for the purchase of eastern forests to protect the headwaters of navigable streams. In 1924, the Clarke-McNary Act empowered the Forest Service to purchase all types of forestlands, regardless of their alleged importance to the protection of navigable waterways. Initially, only 2 million acres were acquired under the provisions of the Weeks Act; today, however, the national forests of the East total more than 25 million acres of government land. Unquestionably, much as Theodore Roosevelt's broad interpretation of the Forest Reserve Act of 1891 assured maximum levels of protection for government timber in the West, so the Clarke-McNary Act was crucial to the realization of federal forests in the East.

However, like the national grasslands (now also an important extension of the national forest idea), most forests in the East were rarely covered with their original vegetation. The object of extending the national forest system to the eastern United States—and eventually to threatened grasslands across the prairies and plains—was to restore and revi-

This official photograph of the supervisor's office, Apache National Forest, Arizona, in 1912, subtly conveys the message back to headquarters in Washington, D.C., that the supervisor understands the importance of frugality. Two horses and a sheet of plywood are sufficing for a new desk or table. National Archives (95G-14700A).

talize those long-abused lands. As a common expression has since put it, these were "the lands that nobody else wanted." The pattern of acquisition, in retrospect, was very similar to that adopted by New York State in 1885 for the restoration of the Adirondacks. Through tax foreclosures, abandonment, or outright purchase, private lands in denuded areas were gradually consolidated under government ownership. As government control increased, restoration and management programs were planned and inaugurated. Now, three-quarters of a century later, the success of those programs is dramatically visible in the tens of thousands of square miles that otherwise would have remained as wasted and unproductive lands.

Over the last quarter century, the national forest system has also been connected with another great milestone of conservation, the approval in 1964 of the Wilderness Preservation Act. At the instant of its passage, 9 million acres across the national forest system, principally in the West, were designated as wilderness, "where man is only a visitor and does not remain." Generally associated with the national parks, the wilderness movement in fact drew its most significant inspiration from the national forests. Aldo Leopold and Robert Marshall, the concept's acknowledged pioneers, began their careers as Forest Service rangers. It was Leopold, for example, who persuaded the agency, in 1924, to administer large portions of the Gila National Forest in New Mexico as a wilderness preserve. Many similar designations followed throughout the national forest system until, forty years later, the Wilderness Act itself

Political cartoon, signed "Terry," pen and ink on paper, 17 x 11½.
From the first, special interests in the West protested the administration of public lands, and western congressmen often resisted the creation of national forests. As this 1908 cartoon illustrates, resistance was not necessarily led by the timber industry which logged mostly private and state lands anyway. Western livestock growers had begun to consider grazing on the public domain as a right of first use. Courtesy of the USDA Forest Service, Grey Towers National Historic Landmark.

The lookout tree on Bull Hill, Lassen National Forest, California, September 1912. National Archives negative (95G-12410A). Like the forest ranger, the fire tower is an indelible symbol of America's national forests, suggesting vigilance, isolation, and Yankee ingenuity. Early fire towers were simply platforms perched high on the trunks of standing trees.

It is September 1912, and Jay's Roost lookout tower has just been completed in Wyoming's Medicine Bow National Forest. At first glance, however, the new tower hardly seems more elaborate—or safer—than makeshift ones originally fashioned from large standing trees. National Archives (95G-15331).

was finally approved. That meant legal as well as administrative standing for each designated wilderness; the point is that the Forest Service, if only by administrative initiative, had pioneered wilderness preservation long before such preservation, in its popularity, also became identified with other lands and federal agencies.

Wilderness may not have altered the reputation of the national forests as a primary source of raw materials; it does, however, further testify to the flexibility and depth of the national forest idea. Among its

In a scene typical throughout the West, beds of western yellow pine are carefully attended at the McCloud Nursery, Shasta National Forest, California, in 1914, for the eventual restocking of nearby logging sites. In the estimation of the Forest Service, there could hardly be more dramatic proof of its lasting commitment to the replenishment and perpetuation of all government forest lands. National Archives (95G-19421A).

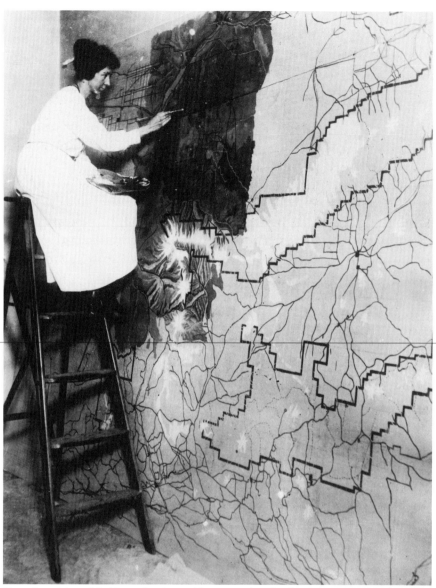

Since the origins of the Forest Service, public outreach to local communities in and near the national forests has included displays, exhibitions, and parade floats, generally associated with holiday celebrations and annual county fairs. Assisting in the preparation of another community project, Helen Dowe, a lookout at the Pike National Forest, Colorado, begins painting a large relief map of the forest for permanent display in the lounge of one of Pueblo's leading hotels. National Archives (95G-152253).

committed advocates, the wilderness concept is perhaps the deepest expression of the nobility and spirituality of the American landscape and thus forms the strongest possible bond between the nation's past and present.

Characterized by long periods of isolation, the life of the forest ranger continues to evoke unforgettable images of hardship and self-sacrifice. This sign at the Gallatin National Forest, Montana, June 24, 1921, subtly appeals to those images, suggesting that only public vigilance will help relieve the forest guards of their lonely and constant daily burden. National Archives (95G-154055).

But again, before anyone could redirect the national forest idea, the forests themselves had to be firmly in place. Basically, four American presidents—and one above the other three—assured that the national forest system would be large enough and diverse enough to accommodate further change and redirection. Thanks to four presidents, and especially to one whose pen was never dry, the American people are still co-owners of the greater proportion of their western forest heritage. All those who now celebrate that heritage will agree—every lingering debate about its purpose and future is, in the end, only further proof of its durability and significance.

A lookout standing guard above McCloud Nursery, Shasta National Forest, California, 1914. Note the American flag and the shadowy profile of Mount Shasta. National Archives negative (95G-19412A).

The Origins and Purposes of the National Forests

by Harold K. Steen

Historians had long agreed on the general account of how the national forests began and how they were to be used. But two fairly recent events outside of the academy sent scholars back to the libraries and archives to take another look. Ironically, historians had always focused on the activities of the executive and legislative branches of government, whereas it was the judiciary that would address penetrating and fundamental questions about the national forests. In 1973, the U.S. District Court in West Virginia decided *Izaak Walton* v. *Butz* in favor of the plaintiff—the so-called Monongahela decision—and in 1978 the U.S. Supreme Court favored the defendant in *U.S.* v. *New Mexico*—the Rio Membres case—and all bets were off. Not only was management of the basic timber and water resources in question, but overall multiple-use policies came under review. The jury is still out on the national forests, and it is timely to refresh our memories on just what Congress intended.

The nineteenth century was a time of drama for America's public lands. Through a myriad of statutes granting land to settlers, incentives to railroads, and dowry to newly admitted states, fully one-half of the nation was transferred from federal ownership to state and private, and the tempo was to continue well into the twentieth century. But as the frontier moved from the humid East to the arid West, scientists and many in government felt increasing concern not only that incomparably rich natural resources were being squandered but also that western settlers and industries had too little water to sustain development. Water was vital for irrigation and river-based commerce, and the link between forested watersheds and water supplies was well-enough understood to prompt a concerted effort to somehow protect forests from destruction. It was this effort that led to the 1891 creation of the National Forest System.

For a nation weaned on the notion that privately owned land was the best kind and one addicted to disposal after a century of wholesale bequests of the land base, it was very difficult to deflect the trajectory and retain selected forested watersheds on the federal ledger. During the last three decades of the nineteenth century, Congress sifted and considered nearly two hundred bills concerning protection of forests on the public domain. Of this amount, only a handful gained enough support to be signed into law, and of the handful, only two were of significance. But two were enough to establish and manage the National Forest System without significant change until the 1960s and 1970s, when the nation reexamined many of its institutions and implemented changes of course.

The first of the two was signed into law on March 3, 1891, authorizing the president to reserve forested public-domain lands from settlement. However, the law contained no statement of purpose for these forested reserves, and Congress set out to correct that deficiency. As before, there was a range of philosophies included in the bills under consideration; the major issue was whether Congress should provide prescriptive legislation or should delegate broad authority to the executive branch. There was some, but not much, debate over whether the resources should be used for homes and commerce, with "use" receiving overwhelming support. There was more debate over whether timber should be cut at all, giving priority to watershed protection, but in the end timber too was to be "used." Finally, water was debated even more than timber; should it be the primary resource and be made available perhaps even to the detriment of other resources? The June 4, 1897, law states that the purpose of these forests is to secure favorable conditions of water flow and future supplies of timber. Land that contained valuable mineral resources or that was more valuable for agriculture than for forest purposes was to be excluded from the reserve system.

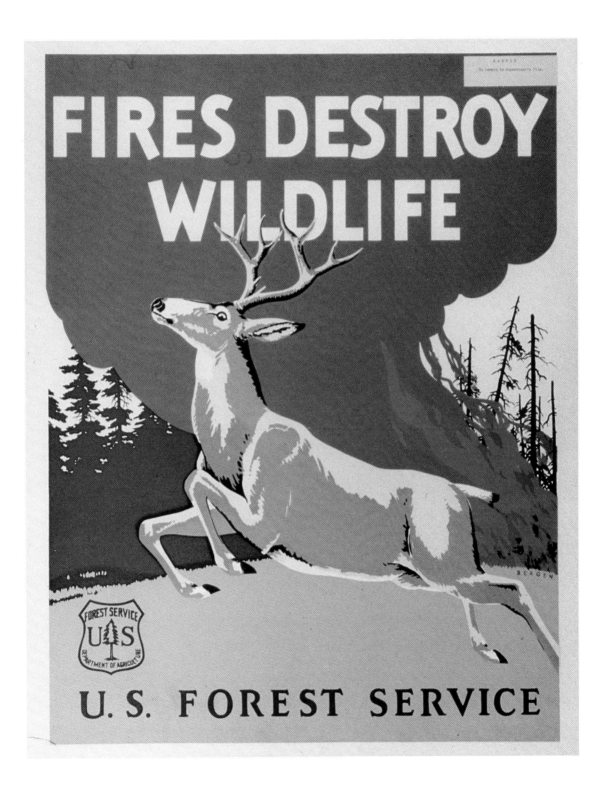

Above as well as preceding and opposite page:
Closely allied with the vision of the national forests as perpetual sources of timber and fresh water has been the notion that all fire is a menace to forest resources. The Forest Service's colorful poster series originally called on a broad range of fear and emotion—suggesting death, patriotism, and foreign aggression—to impress on Americans the importance of guarding their woodlands against arson of every kind.

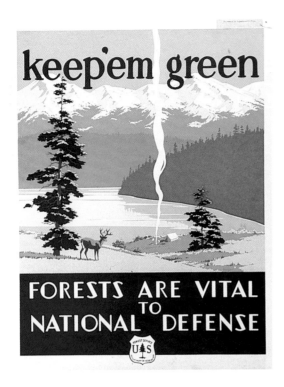

Of course, there were people involved—scientists in and out of the executive branch and politicians in Congress—and their names are familiar to historians. Of the scientists, George Perkins Marsh stands a head above the others, for it was he, as early as 1864, who warned of environmental abuse and advanced concepts of land ethics and sustainable development. John Wesley Powell, the western explorer and ethnographer, in 1888 headed the Irrigation Survey, the agency that articulated water scarcity in the arid West and insisted that protection of forests was essential to water supply. Arnold Hague, Powell's lieutenant, being more

A fire toolbox located on the divide between the Hayden and Routt national forests (now the Medicine Bow and Routt, bordering Wyoming and Colorado), June 1912. Hundreds of similar photographs were forwarded to Forest Service officials in Washington, D.C., as proof that management directives to prepare for fire fighting had in fact been carried out. National Archives (95G-11603A).

Opposite page:
Albert Staehle painted the first Smokey Bear in 1944. Subsequent posters were painted by the Forest Service artist Rudy Wendelin from 1949 until his retirement in 1973. By 1952, Smokey was so famous that Congress passed legislation prohibiting the use of his image without the permission of the Forest Service. Under the auspices of The Advertising Council of America, Smokey nonetheless has spoken for the protection of America's forests, parks, and private lands at large. All posters courtesy of the National Archives.

of a scientist and less of a politician, survived a fickle Congress when Powell did not and assured a flow of hard data into the process. W. J. McGee, also with the Irrigation Survey and the most literate scientist of them all, expertly wrote of forest-water relationships. A scientist to the core, G. K. Gilbert reported on water's relation to land forms with such rigor that late-nineteenth-century America led the world in the field of geology. Finally, Bernhard E. Fernow, the nation's first technically trained forester and the chief of the federal forestry agency, was able to meld the biological properties of the forest with the physical characteristics of the land and, through his reports and testimony, keep Congress apprised.

Politicians are a little harder to track than the scientists because they produced few, if any, signed reports, but a few clearly deserve recognition for their contribution to national forest history. Congressman Mark Dunnell of Minnesota was key in the 1876 establishment of a federal forestry program. Three years earlier he had sponsored the ill-fated Timber Culture Act, which linked reforestation with climate change, an idea that has regained popular favor in modern times. Congressman

Cooperative fire-fighting arrangements on the national forests included working with the major railroads whose main lines abutted or crossed government lands. This Southern Pacific fire train, based at Donner Summit, California, pumped 350 gallons per minute from two tank cars holding 25,000 gallons each. Four such trains were based on the Southern Pacific main line across the Sierra Nevada. National Archives photograph (95G-190594).

Thomas McRae of Arkansas was the primary author of the 1897 statute that determined the purpose of the national forests. Senator Richard Pettigrew of South Dakota materially helped McRae's bill to passage by first dropping opposition to it and then supporting it. Names of other politicians, usually chairmen of leading congressional committees, also appear in historical accounts of the national forests, but recent scholarship has turned up Congressman William Holman of Indiana. Holman is important because he provided key language for the 1891 Forest Reserve Act and also the legislative trail that enables us to learn more about the original congressional intent.

It was this intent that the courts interpreted in the 1970s, causing very significant changes in the ways the national forests are managed. The 1973 *Izaak Walton* v. *Butz* struck down clear-cutting, with the recommendation that a new law be enacted. Congress responded in 1976 with the National Forest Management Act, which legalized clear-cutting under certain conditions. This was also a prescriptive measure, reversing the broad management mandate included in the 1897 law. The Supreme Court's 1978 *U.S.* v. *New Mexico* decision determined that maintaining timber and water supplies was the only true purpose of national forests and that other uses were subordinate. The decision further brought into question basic water rights throughout the arid West, a question that will take years to answer fully.

The heroic image of the forest ranger has itself contributed to the esthetic ideal of the classical forest, as demonstrated by this wonderfully understated photograph taken in Logan Canyon, Utah, Cache (now Wasatch-Cache) National Forest, 1914. National Archives (95G-21043A).

The Classical Forest

The longer an institution lasts, the more likely it is to be woven into a society's collective consciousness. The disadvantage of longevity is the tendency to forget—or even to dismiss as unimportant or irrelevant—some of the guiding principles that probably inspired that institution's evolution in the first place. At that point, Harold K. Steen has reminded us, some scholar or the courts may intervene, restoring, in the process, a more complete and accurate picture of the institution's founding ideals and legal obligations.

The controversies that currently grip the national forests may be traced, in large part, to elements of indifference to the historical record. Many environmentalists, for example, have long tended to dismiss the contributions of the national forests solely because the forests are associated with production. Nor have environmentalists ever forgiven Gifford Pinchot for siding with development on all public-land issues, and especially for supporting the city of San Francisco in the infamous Hetch Hetchy debate. As early as 1901, San Francisco had petitioned the federal government for permission to dam the Hetch Hetchy Valley, despite the fact that it was inside the boundary of Yosemite National Park. Preservationists were incensed by the petition, noting that Hetch Hetchy was another "crown jewel" of the American landscape, a replica of Yosemite Valley itself. City officials argued that if the nation already had one Yosemite Valley, what need was there for two? Gifford Pinchot agreed, testifying that Hetch Hetchy's so-called highest and best use was to provide limitless stores of fresh water for hundreds of thousands of urban residents. In 1913 Congress took a vote and by wide margins in

Established during the depths of the Great Depression in 1933, the Civilian Conservation Corps was seen as an opportunity to restore both people and the American land. Extensive works of restoration occurred throughout the national forests. Here young men plant seedlings on a forestry and soil erosion project in eastern Tennessee, January 1935. Courtesy of the Forest History Society.

both houses upheld San Francisco. Shortly afterward, Hetch Hetchy passed over to the control of city engineers.

Unfortunately, in their indignation toward Gifford Pinchot for having supported the realignment of a major national park, preservationists also quickly soured on the national forest idea. "There is no one but you and I," Charles Sprague Sargent bitterly complained to John Muir, for example, "who really love the North American trees." No less convinced of the correctness of their own position, career administrators of the Forest Service sought to make the forests "pay." Lost, in either case, was much of the original promise of the national forest idea, specifically, the pledge that the system was intended not only to secure the country's means of production but also to protect the American landscape as a source of national pride. Pinchot, of course, vehemently disputed every contention that by supporting the Hetch Hetchy dam, he had compromised that commitment. How could the development of any natural resource be viewed as destructive, he argued, if its use was fully consistent with sustained-yield methodologies?

Once again, it is regrettable, if understandable, that so many environmentalists have dismissed the sincerity of his observation. Simply, Pinchot had been schooled in the European forest model, which, to his

Early efforts to convince critics that the national forests were indeed for recreation, and not just intensive logging, included the new entrance arch to the Denny Creek Camp Ground, Snoqualmie National Forest, Washington, 1919. National Archives (95G-44237A)

mind, *was* both beautiful and functional. Trees were never "cleared"; rather they were "thinned." Even as some trees were coming down, many more were always growing. By being consistently selective, in other words, the forester could not help but remain sensitive to the natural environment as a whole.

As the principal founder of the Wilderness Society in 1935, Robert Marshall has often been called the father of wilderness preservation. Like his renowned contemporary, Aldo Leopold, Marshall was inspired by several tours of duty in the U.S. Forest Service. Courtesy of the Forest History Society.

The evolving contention that the classical forest model was old-fashioned and inefficient—especially in even-aged stands of a single tree species—therefore became the ultimate hindrance to maintaining the historical alliance between landscape esthetics and the national forest idea. There remained, in addition, the lingering mistrust over the loss of Hetch Hetchy. Consequently, whatever the Forest Service proposed was likely to be viewed with suspicion. Begrudgingly, preservationists acknowledged the contributions of Aldo Leopold and Robert Marshall (among others), who, despite their allegiance to the principles of sustained-yield forestry, also broke from the absolutism of the majority of their peers by declaring that millions of acres of the national forests should never be touched. The wilderness concept, in its commitment to full protection, squared readily with the views of preservationists. Even so, the most vocal were still reluctant to give any credit to the Forest Service—and

Aldo Leopold, by Robert McCabe.
Courtesy of the Forest History Society.

thus indirectly to Gifford Pinchot—for having laid the foundations of
wilderness protection in the first place by aggressively promoting the
expansion of the original forest system.

Sacrificed, as a final result, was a deeper public understanding of
the importance of the national forests as a crucible of American conservation. To the vast majority of Americans, the story of conservation is
the history of the national parks, as told, for example, through the writ-
ings of John Muir. Otherwise, the public lands are all a blur, a jumble of
agencies and seemingly overlapping jurisdictions. It is small wonder that
the general public is often confused and, in that confusion, has gradually lost touch with the distinctiveness of the national forest idea.

If history is any guide, the way back to public understanding leads
to the classical forest model. "A thing is right when it tends to preserve
the integrity, stability, and beauty of the biotic community," Aldo Leopold

once observed. "It is wrong when it tends otherwise." The alternative argument has failed the test of history as well as of esthetics. Even if appearances are deceiving—even if the residual ugliness of exploitation will eventually heal—questions remain: How long will it take and at what final price? "Quit thinking about decent land-use as solely an economic problem," Leopold further advised. "Examine each question in terms of what is ethically and esthetically right, as well as what is economically expedient."

That may never have been the reality of the national forests; it most definitely, however, is their historical ideal. The early prophets of conservation promised agelessness through consistency. There would be wholesome forests everywhere, *wholesome* defined as functional *and* beautiful. After all, it was not as if a human being could postpone the inevitable. No one should sacrifice years—sacrifice more of *life*—to await the return of a forest that was also pleasing to the eye. Indeed, in paintings, pictures, and other office memorabilia, the Forest Service itself has confessed, if only subconsciously, that it is the classical—and not the consumptive—forest model that stirs the soul.

Summer cabins in the national forests, such as this one overlooking portions of the Pisgah National Forest (North Carolina and Tennessee) and photographed in 1930, have periodically testified to the sincerity of official attempts to maintain a traditional forest landscape. National Archives (95G-238076).

Thus we come back to the durability of culture, to the need for reconciling modern management with historical ideals. And some might say that a reconciliation has already occurred. The Wilderness Preservation Act of 1964; the designation of hundreds of thousands of additional acres of public forests as national recreation areas; the protection of wild and scenic rivers; and the evolution of yet another category, national *scenic* areas—all testify that the Forest Service has become increasingly involved in the protection of landscape esthetics. As before, the challenge is how to extend that level of sensitivity to encompass the national forests as a whole rather than to limit biological and esthetic responsibility to those restricted categories.

Understandably, the Forest Service still sees itself as the arbiter of such issues. And one way to arbitrate is to subdivide the resource, assigning, in effect, each special interest its private sphere of influence. The method is most often challenged for risking the dilution of the resource as a whole. Thus the rejection of classical forestry, however circumspect or limited, may be said to have pitted the aims of modern management against the ideal of a holistic landscape.

To Forest Service claims that the agency is more aware—that it is, even today, a more effective sounding board for environmental questions—the historian can respond only with past words of caution. It is simply too early to tell how the most recent commitments will eventually turn out. What the historian can say with certainty is that the opportunity has been preserved. The privilege of changing direction is still within the nation's grasp. And ideally, for as long as the forests endure, the opportunity should endure also.

Which, then, will it be: a system of management that tends to fragment or compartmentalize so-called competing natural values or, as originally promised, working forests that are universally functional, beautiful, and ecologically sound? No doubt, it is a challenging decision. But is it really impossible to make? Throughout history, at least, the latter is the kind of forest—and forest management—most Americans have said they want. Ultimately, it therefore stands to reason, that forest is the only kind they will accept.

Frederic Remington, *The Roundup*, oil on canvas, 27 x 40; Buffalo Bill Historical Center.

A Note on the Sources

In any history of the national forests, it is common to expect a checklist detailing, in particular, the evolution of the Forest Service and its chief administrative tenets. Few books or articles seriously attempt the opposite, that is, retain as their primary focus the national forest idea. The following is intended merely as an introduction to the literature, although again, the reader is asked to bear in mind the distinction between cultural and administrative history.

An excellent point of departure that includes both historical perspectives is Richard C. Davis, ed., *Encyclopedia of American Forest and Conservation History*, 2 vols. (New York: Macmillan Publishing Company, 1983). Also relevant are Richard C. Davis, ed., *North American Forest History: A Guide to Archives and Manuscripts in the United States and Canada*, and Ronald J. Fahl, ed., *North American Forest and Conservation History: A Bibliography*, both published in 1977 by the Forest History Society in conjunction with A.B.C.-Clio Press, Santa Barbara, California. Relevant updates of these bibliographies appear regularly in *Forest and Conservation History* (formerly the *Journal of Forest History*). Merely relying on these three reference works should introduce the general reader or prospective researcher to better than 90 percent of the available secondary works and primary source materials.

For nearly a half century, the standard scholarly study of forests in America was John Ise, *The United States Forest Policy* (New Haven: Yale University Press, 1920). Ise's work has since been supplanted by a broad variety of research monographs, among them Richard G. Lilliard, *The Great Forest* (New York: Alfred A. Knopf, 1947); Thomas R. Cox et al.,

This Well-Wooded Land: Americans and Their Forests from Colonial Times to the Present (Lincoln: University of Nebraska Press, 1985); Michael Frome, *Whose Woods These Are: The Story of the National Forests* (Garden City, N.Y.: Doubleday, 1962); and David A. Clary, *Timber and the Forest Service* (Lawrence: University of Kansas Press, 1986). A definitive account of the Forest Service is Harold K. Steen, *The U.S. Forest Service: A History* (Seattle: University of Washington Press, 1976). Also relevant are Michael Frome, *The Forest Service*, 2d rev. ed. (Boulder: Westview Press, 1984), and Glen O. Robinson, *The Forest Service: A Study in Public Land Management* (Baltimore: Johns Hopkins University Press, 1975).

The classic account of the relationship of the forestry movement to American conservation at large is Samuel P. Hays, *Conservation and the Gospel of Efficiency: The Progressive Conservation Movement, 1890–1920* (Cambridge: Harvard University Press, 1959). Readers will also want to consult Hays's latest volume, *Beauty, Health, and Permanence: Environmental Politics in the United States, 1955–1985* (New York: Cambridge University Press, 1987), which, like this volume, attempts to place the national forest idea in a wider social context. Stephen Fox, *John Muir and His Legacy: The American Conservation Movement* (Boston: Little, Brown, 1981), is also excellent for describing the historical tensions between advocates for the consumption of natural resources and those for the protection of natural beauty. Also seminal in this regard is Roderick Nash, *Wilderness and the American Mind*, 3d rev. ed. (New Haven: Yale University Press, 1982); Hans Huth, *Nature and the American: Three Centuries of Changing Attitudes* (Berkeley and Los Angeles: University of California Press, 1957); Barbara Novak, *Nature and Culture: American Landscape and Painting, 1825–1875* (New York and Toronto: Oxford University Press, 1980); Leo Marx, *The Machine in the Garden: Technology and the Pastoral Ideal in America* (New York: Oxford University Press, 1964); and Douglas H. Strong, *Dreamers and Defenders: American Conservationists* (Lincoln: University of Nebraska Press, 1988).

The definitive history of forest protection is Stephen H. Pyne, *Fire in America: A Cultural History of Wildland and Rural Fire* (Princeton: Princeton University Press, 1982). John F. Reiger takes a different departure in *American Sportsmen and the Origins of Conservation* (New York: Winchester Press, 1975), arguing that sportsmen were every bit as important as foresters and preservationists in seeking the protection of the national parks and national forests. Regardless of that debate, no one disagrees that the national forest system measurably inspired one of America's greatest wildlife advocates, Aldo Leopold. His classic *A Sand*

County Almanac (New York: Oxford University Press, 1949), released just after his death, is perhaps the single most important statement on conservation ethics ever published in the United States.

Finally, even a brief bibliography such as this would be incomplete without Gifford Pinchot's *Breaking New Ground* (New York: Harcourt, Brace and Company, 1947). Although very opinionated and at times self-congratulatory, these memoirs are indeed a lively and important introduction to the founding ideals of the national forest system. Readers will simply want to consult the major bibliographies listed at the outset, as well as the many excellent sources cited in the secondary literature, for contrasting views and opinions about Pinchot and his role in the U.S. Forest Service.

As the national forest idea officially enters its second century, undoubtedly a new generation of scholars will probe its founding ideals, proof again that the mere existence of the national forests is perhaps the greatest testimony to their enduring significance.

ABOUT THE AUTHOR

Alfred Runte is a self-employed public historian and author living in Seattle. Among other books on public lands, he is the author of *Trains of Discovery: Western Railroads and the National Parks*, published by Roberts Rinehart in 1990.